Original title:
Love's Labor

Copyright © 2024 Swan Charm
All rights reserved.

Author: Johan Kirsipuu
ISBN HARDBACK: 978-9916-86-752-5
ISBN PAPERBACK: 978-9916-86-753-2
ISBN EBOOK: 978-9916-86-754-9

Seasons of Togetherness

In spring we bloomed, hand in hand,
With laughter bright, we filled the land.
Summer's sun, our smiles did trace,
In golden light, we found our place.

As autumn leaves began to fall,
We gathered close, we felt the call.
The winter's chill could not divide,
For by each other's side, we bide.

Letters Never Sent

In quiet nights, I wrote in vain,
Words wrapped in hope, yet soaked in pain.
Each letter filled with dreams unshared,
A heart in silence, too scared, too bared.

The ink now dries on pages grey,
Stories lost, where whispers sway.
Yet deep inside, the truth's still bright,
These letters hold my love, my light.

Crafting a Future

With hands entwined, we sketch our dreams,
In vibrant colors, life redeems.
Together we paint the skies so wide,
And map our journey, side by side.

Through storms and shadows, we will stand,
With courage bold, like grains of sand.
Each moment woven, a tapestry,
In crafting a future, just you and me.

Echoes of Hearts

In every heartbeat, a story flows,
A rhythm shared, where love bestows.
The echoes dance in twilight's glow,
Reminders sweet of what we know.

Through valleys low and mountains high,
Our hearts will soar, they will not lie.
In whispered dreams and gentle sighs,
The echoes of love will never die.

Torn Pages of Our Journey

We wandered through the night,
With shadows as our guide,
Each step a silent plea,
In dreams, we would confide.

The ink began to fade,
As laughter filled the air,
Memories like whispers,
Softly leading us there.

Through valleys deep we trod,
With burdens yet unseen,
Our hearts became the map,
Every turn a new glean.

In storms we found our strength,
United, hand in hand,
With every tear that fell,
We learned to understand.

Now pages turn to dust,
Yet stories linger on,
In the chapters yet to write,
Our journey's never gone.

The Dance of Two Souls

In moonlight, we converge,
Like rivers to the sea,
With every step we take,
We write our melody.

Your laughter is a tune,
That plays within my heart,
Each glance, a fleeting note,
In this dance, we won't part.

As stars begin to fade,
We twirl through silent nights,
Two souls in perfect sync,
Embracing all delights.

The world around us blurs,
As time begins to slow,
In the rhythm of our love,
Together, we will grow.

Each heartbeat echoes love,
A symphony so rare,
In this dance of souls,
A bond beyond compare.

In the Forge of Togetherness

In the quiet of the night,
We hammer dreams anew,
With every spark of hope,
Our vision comes in view.

The heat of shared desires,
Transforms the iron will,
As we shape our future,
With passion, strong and still.

Through trials, we endure,
United by our trust,
In the embers of our fight,
We find love's golden crust.

With every blow we strike,
New patterns start to form,
In the forge of our hearts,
We weather every storm.

Together, we stand tall,
As legends born in fire,
In this sacred space,
We fulfill our heart's desire.

A Symphony of Shared Moments

Each moment shared with you,
Is music to my soul,
In laughter, in the tears,
We find our perfect whole.

Like notes upon a score,
We harmonize so sweet,
In every glance exchanged,
Our hearts skip with the beat.

The world becomes a stage,
As we dance through the day,
Creating our own rhythm,
In a bright, shimmering way.

With memories we compose,
A melody divine,
In this symphony of love,
Your heart forever mine.

As time unfolds its wings,
We'll sing our truths aloud,
In this life of shared moments,
Together, forever proud.

Notes on a Frayed Page

Words once bright, now faded,
Whispers trapped in time's embrace.
Ink spills secrets, half-truths,
Lost moments in a silent space.

Curled edges, softening dreams,
Each crease holds a story dear.
Fingers trace forgotten schemes,
A testament to love and fear.

Memories dance in the margins,
Laughter echoes through the night.
Each note, a spark of passion,
Guiding through the darkest flight.

Reflections in a Moonlit Pond

Silver ripples greet the night,
Stars whisper from above.
Moonlight drips like gentle rain,
Caressing depths where shadows love.

Time slows down in tranquil waves,
Secrets linger on the breeze.
Nature's heart quietly craves,
Harmony among the trees.

Thoughts float softly on the surface,
Boundless dreams meet starlit eyes.
In this place, free from pretense,
The soul finds peace, where stillness lies.

A Journey without a Destination

Footsteps echo on the ground,
Paths unworn, yet full of grace.
With each step, new sights are found,
Wandering gives a joyful chase.

The horizon beckons softly,
Whispers of the road ahead.
Every turn brings something wealthy,
Unfolding tales of life unsaid.

In this endless stream of time,
Every heartbeat tells the way.
Boundless skies and mountains climb,
Adventure blooms in the light of day.

The Echo of Your Laughter

In the air, your laughter lingers,
A melody, sweet and rare.
Like a song that gently lingers,
Spreading joy, erasing care.

Through the halls, it dances lightly,
Casting shadows near and far.
Every chuckle sparks so brightly,
A reminder of who you are.

In my heart, your spirit glows,
Resonating in the night.
Echoing where the wind blows,
Filling silence with delight.

The Garden of Our Hopes

In a patch of sunlight,
Seeds of dreams take root,
With water from our laughter,
And sunbeams as our loot.

Petals of bright colors,
Whispering sweet delight,
Each bloom a small promise,
In the soft morning light.

Breezes carry stories,
Of the love we once knew,
In this garden we tend,
All our hopes feel anew.

Time it gently brushes,
Through leaves that dance and sway,
Together we'll keep planting,
Our tomorrows today.

Through the days that wander,
We'll find our paths entwined,
In this garden of hopes,
Forever intertwined.

Between the Lines of an Old Letter

In faded ink and paper,
A tale of love once shared,
Words hold the weight of longing,
In each sentence, love bared.

A heart laid bare in verses,
With secrets softly told,
Memories bound in pages,
As the past starts to unfold.

Between the lines of laughter,
And whispers of despair,
A connection still lingers,
In the words we laid bare.

Each crease tells a story,
Of the times we once knew,
Between the lines of silence,
An echo of me and you.

Though time may sweep us onward,
And the world spins so fast,
Those letters hold the magic,
Of a love that will last.

Wishes Adrift on a Breeze

In the quiet of twilight,
Wishes float on the air,
Like whispers of the evening,
Spreading dreams everywhere.

Stars blink in the distance,
A canvas dark and deep,
While hopes sail on the horizon,
Where the night shadows creep.

Each wish a gentle flutter,
Twirling through the sweet night,
Adrift in the soft silence,
Chasing after the light.

With every breath of nighttime,
Our dreams take to the skies,
As wishes dance on breezes,
In the dark they arise.

Let them soar like feathers,
On winds so wild and free,
For in the heart of dreaming,
Lies the truth we all see.

The Poetry of Intent

In the ink of intention,
Words form like morning dew,
Each thought, a fresh beginning,
With a purpose to pursue.

Lines crafted with intent,
Awaken dreams to flight,
Rhymes that weave our stories,
In the tapestry of night.

Every verse holds a candle,
Illuminating the way,
Guiding us through shadows,
To the dawn of each day.

In the heart of creation,
We're sculptors of our fate,
With the poetry of intent,
We shape what love can sate.

So let our voices gather,
In a chorus strong and clear,
For in the art of living,
Intentions persevere.

The Garden of Together

In the sunlit glade we stand,
Hands entwined, hearts expand.
Flowers bloom, colors bright,
Together we weave pure light.

In whispers soft, secrets shared,
A bond that's nurtured, a love declared.
With every seed that we sow,
Our garden thrives, love will grow.

Branches sway under the sky,
In this space, we learn to fly.
Time may pass with fleeting grace,
In our haven, we embrace.

Breezes carry laughter's song,
In unity, we find where we belong.
Moments captured, treasured dear,
In this garden, we shall not fear.

Through storms and shadows that arrive,
Together, we will always thrive.
Our roots run deep, intertwined,
In this garden, love defined.

The Intersection of Souls

Where paths converge, a spark ignites,
In the silence, truth ignites.
Two worlds collide, hearts align,
In this moment, the stars define.

Eyes that speak, no words need be,
Understanding flows, wild and free.
In every glance, a story unfolds,
A tapestry of warmth that holds.

With every heartbeat, rhythms blend,
In the dance of souls, we transcend.
Echoes linger, whispers near,
At this junction, love draws near.

Moments shared, a sacred trust,
In vulnerability, we are just.
The tie that binds, deep yet light,
Guided forward, souls take flight.

In this place, the world feels right,
Together we rise, an endless height.
To dance in shadows, to laugh, to weep,
In the intersection, our hearts leap.

Building Bridges with Care

Stone by stone, we lay each path,
With gentle hands, we bridge the gaps.
Through storms and trials, we design,
Structures strong, where hearts align.

In patience forged, with love embraced,
Walls of worry, we replace.
Each step taken, trust refined,
In this journey, hope intertwined.

With every plank and sturdy beam,
Connections made, we dare to dream.
Together we rise, sturdy and fair,
In this labor, we find our prayer.

Through rivers wide and valleys deep,
In this bond, our promises keep.
Crafting pathways, hand in hand,
A testament to understand.

With every bridge, we pave the way,
A testament to love's bright ray.
In unity, we share and care,
Building bridges, hearts laid bare.

The Pulse of Commitment

In quietude we pledge our hearts,
With every spark, our journey starts.
Through trials faced, we stand as one,
In every dawn, our song's begun.

The weight we lift, the dreams we chase,
In sacred trust, we find our place.
With steady hands, we boldly steer,
In every beat, our love is clear.

Through stormy skies and gentle rain,
Our bond remains, a steadfast chain.
Each whisper soft, each glance aligned,
In moments shared, our souls entwined.

We carve our path with strength and grace,
In every turn, we find our space.
With every choice, our futures blend,
In the pulse of commitment, we transcend.

An Ode to Us

Together we bloom in vibrant hues,
In laughter shared, we chase the blues.
With every glance, a story unfolds,
In every hug, a warmth that holds.

We dance through life, two souls in flight,
In whispered dreams, we find our light.
Through trials faced, we stand so tall,
In unity, we conquer all.

Hand in hand, we weave our tales,
In every stride, love never fails.
Through seasons' change, our hearts remain,
In joy and sorrow, we share the pain.

Each moment cherished, a treasure rare,
In our embrace, the world feels fair.
An ode to us, forever true,
In the depths of love, there's always you.

A Shared Horizon

Upon the rise of each new day,
We chase the sun, not far away.
With dreams that stretch beyond the sky,
In unison, we learn to fly.

Through mountains high and valleys low,
In every step, our spirits glow.
Together charting paths unknown,
In every heartbeat, we have grown.

The colors blend, our futures bright,
In unity, we find our light.
With every glance, two souls align,
In love's embrace, our stars will shine.

As waves caress the sandy shore,
In every moment, we crave more.
With hands held tight, we'll stand as one,
A shared horizon, our journey begun.

The Space Between Heartbeats

In the silence where love resides,
A gentle pulse, where hope abides.
In quiet moments, souls unite,
In every sigh, sparks ignite.

A breathless pause, the world feels still,
In softest whispers, hearts will thrill.
Each heartbeat echoes, a tender song,
In this space, we both belong.

Time dances slow, in serene embrace,
In fleeting glances, we find our pace.
Through every heartbeat, stories rise,
In the spaces, love never lies.

So here's to us in soft twilight,
In the space between, all feels right.
With every pulse, our spirits soar,
In love's own rhythm, forevermore.

Chiseled from the Same Stone

In ancient quarries, hearts were formed,
Two spirits carved, through trials warmed.
Weathered edges, smooth yet strong,
Together resilient, where we belong.

Through storms we've walked, hand in hand,
Reflecting strength in the grains of sand.
Each crack a story, each flaw a sign,
Chiseled together, your heart and mine.

In silent shadows, our laughter rings,
A symphony of life that forever sings.
With love's hammer, we shape our way,
In unity, we brighten each day.

Time may weather, still we stand,
Molding dreams with a tender hand.
In the sculptor's eye, we shine bright,
Chiseled from the same stone, a shared light.

The Palette of Togetherness

Colors blend in a vibrant swirl,
With every stroke, new stories unfurl.
Each hue a moment, a memory bright,
In the canvas of life, we paint our light.

In laughter's gold, in sorrow's gray,
We mix them freely, come what may.
From dawn's soft blush to twilight's teal,
Together we blend, together we heal.

Brush held firm in love's embrace,
Each color chosen, each line we trace.
With shades of joy and tints of woe,
The palette of togetherness starts to glow.

Brushstrokes echo our heart's refrain,
In harmony, we dance through rain.
With every painting, a story we share,
A masterpiece crafted with love and care.

A Bridge Between Souls

In twilight's glow, the bridges rise,
Connecting hearts beneath the skies.
Two paths converge, with gentle grace,
A bridge between souls in a sacred space.

Each step we take, a story unfolds,
With whispered secrets that love beholds.
Together we traverse the unknown,
A bridge between souls, forever grown.

Through rivers of doubt and valleys of fear,
Our bond unbroken, always near.
With faith as our guide and hope as our toll,
We walk on the bridge that links our souls.

In the still of night, let echoes sing,
Of every heartbeat and everything.
For in the silence, our spirits play,
Building a bridge that never fades away.

Pages Bound by Embrace

In the book of life, our story we write,
With every chapter, our dreams take flight.
Each page a turning, a whispering grace,
Bound by embrace in a sacred space.

Ink that dances on paper so white,
Tales of laughter and warmth ignite.
With every word, our hearts entwine,
Pages bound by love, forever mine.

Through storms we scribble, through sunshine we play,
Each plot unfolding in a beautiful way.
In margins, we scribble our hopes and fears,
Bound by embrace across the years.

With every bookmark, reminders we save,
Of moments together, so bold and brave.
In this tome of ours, love always stays,
Pages bound by embrace, through all our days.

Mending Hearts with Every Stitch

With threads of hope we weave,
In colors bright and bold,
Each stitch a gentle touch,
A story yet untold.

Through fabric worn with care,
We patch the frayed apart,
In every pull and tug,
We mend a wounded heart.

Time's needle doth not pause,
Yet, we will not despair,
Together we will mend,
With love beyond compare.

A quilt of shared moments,
Our laughter sewn with tears,
Each piece a testament,
To all our hopes and fears.

So gather 'round the work,
As hands join firm and tight,
In unity we find,
The warmth of love's still light.

Echoes of Intimacy

In whispers soft like rain,
Our secrets find their way,
Each breath a shared intent,
In night that turns to day.

Your laughter dances close,
A melody of trust,
In shadows deep we meet,
The bond that's more than just.

Hearts beat in gentle sync,
With rhythms known so well,
In silence, eyes can speak,
A language we can tell.

In every glance exchanged,
A universe unfolds,
In sweetness, soft and pure,
A story love beholds.

Through echoes of our dreams,
We weave a sacred space,
In intimacy profound,
We find our truest grace.

Sowing Seeds of Connection

In gardens rich with care,
We plant our dreams anew,
With every seed we sow,
A bond begins to bloom.

With sunlight, warmth, and rain,
Connections start to rise,
As roots entwine below,
In love's embrace, we thrive.

We water hope with grace,
And nurture every thought,
Through seasons that we share,
In laughter, pain, and sought.

The harvest of our hearts,
In colors rich and bright,
Through every thorn we pass,
We gather pure delight.

So let us sow with joy,
And watch the flowers grow,
In fields of shared embrace,
The seeds of love we sow.

The Canvas of Our Togetherness

With brushes bold and bright,
We paint our days in hues,
Each stroke a memory,
In colors we can choose.

The canvas laughs and cries,
With every shade we find,
In artistry of souls,
We mirror heart and mind.

Through splashes of our dreams,
We create a vibrant scene,
In every line and curve,
A love that's strong and keen.

Though storms may cloud the view,
We mix our paints with hope,
In every twist and turn,
We learn together, cope.

So let us not forget,
The colors that we share,
On this canvas of life,
Our togetherness laid bare.

Heartstrings and Handshakes

In a crowded room, we stand so close,
Our eyes exchange a silent prose.
A gentle smile, a warm embrace,
Two souls dancing in a shared space.

The world fades, we pause the time,
In this moment, rhythm and rhyme.
Hands connect like melodies sweet,
A symphony where heartbeats meet.

Through laughter and through whispered fears,
We weave our stories across the years.
With every handshake, with every glance,
We find ourselves in a timeless dance.

When shadows loom and doubts arise,
We hold each other, a bond that ties.
With heartstrings pulled, we sail the night,
Together, we find our guiding light.

Hand in hand, we'll face the storm,
In this refuge, we are warm.
With every pulse, a promise sworn,
In heartbeats, our love is born.

The Weight of Silent Affection

In nights so dark, your gaze ignites,
A spark that dances, soft delights.
Words unspoken, yet we know,
In gentle glances, love will grow.

A quiet touch upon my skin,
In that moment, worlds begin.
An echo of the things unsaid,
In silence, all our fears are shed.

The weight of love, a heavy sigh,
In whispered breaths, we say goodbye.
Yet linger close, the warmth remains,
In hearts entwined, we share our pains.

Soft shadows cast where secrets dwell,
In every heartbeat, stories tell.
No need for words, your heart aligns,
This silent bond, a love that shines.

As twilight fades, the stars appear,
In every twinkle, you are near.
Together bound in twilight's hush,
Our silent love, a sacred rush.

Crafting Dreams Together

Under the stars, we sketch our dreams,
With every stroke, your laughter beams.
A canvas bright with hopes in view,
Together crafting visions true.

With hands entwined, we build our fate,
In whispered plans, we celebrate.
Each little wish, a step we take,
An artwork formed with every break.

Through trials tough and skies so gray,
We find our colors, come what may.
With love's embrace, the world we pen,
Crafting chapters again and again.

When dreams take flight, and fears collide,
We chase the stars, hearts open wide.
In every moment, hand in hand,
Together here, we firmly stand.

The future beckons, bold and bright,
With you beside me, I feel the light.
Crafting dreams, our souls aware,
In every heartbeat, we declare.

Bound by Tender Threads

In quiet corners, love is spun,
With gentle threads, our hearts are one.
We weave our stories, hand in hand,
In every knot, a promise stands.

Through every tear and smile we share,
Threads of hope weave in the air.
Embracing joy, while facing pain,
In every stitch, we stitch the gain.

As seasons turn and moments fade,
We hold our bond, unafraid.
With every challenge, we will find,
Tender threads, forever bind.

In laughter's echo and in sighs,
We find our way, beneath the skies.
Bound together, come what may,
In love's embrace, we choose to stay.

The tapestry of life unfolds,
In every shade, the heart beholds.
With tender threads, our lives entwined,
A masterpiece of love defined.

The Tapestry of Yearning

In shadows cast by dreams we weave,
Threads of hope and love that cleave.
Whispers echo in the night,
Longing hearts take flight.

Each stitch holds a silent prayer,
Woven tales of love and care.
Colors blend in soft embrace,
A dance of time, a sacred space.

Through tangled paths of joy and pain,
Golden hues meet silver rain.
In every knot, a story told,
A tapestry of hearts, bold.

Yearning echoes through the years,
Mixed with laughter, mixed with tears.
In the fabric, lives entwined,
A masterpiece of love, defined.

Beneath the stars, our hopes ignite,
In woven threads, we find the light.
The universe, our guiding thread,
A tapestry where dreams are fed.

Where Hearts Converge

In the silence where whispers meet,
Two souls find their sacred seat.
Eyes that shine with truths unspoken,
In this space, hearts are broken.

Beneath the moon's soft silver glow,
Words like rivers gently flow.
Hands entwined, a silent vow,
In this moment, love to plow.

The world outside fades away,
In this union, night and day.
Threaded dreams, a perfect blend,
In each heartbeat, love transcends.

Through laughter shared and sorrow too,
In the chaos, we find our cue.
Where hearts converge, we lose the fight,
Wrapped in warmth, lost in light.

Here in this place, time stands still,
With every breath, we dare to feel.
A sanctuary where we belong,
Together, forever, love so strong.

The Alchemy of Vulnerability

In fragile spaces, truth emerges,
A dance of heart, where love converges.
With every scar, a story shines,
In vulnerability, strength entwines.

To open up, to risk the fall,
In this courage, we find our call.
Sharing shadows, light breaks through,
In the rawness, we find the true.

Trust like gold, forged in fire,
Crafting bonds that rise higher.
With every tear, we learn to grow,
In the depths, our spirits flow.

Embracing flaws, the beauty lies,
In every flaw, the heart replies.
The alchemy of souls laid bare,
Transforming pain into love's care.

As petals fall, we stand as one,
In the twilight, we see the sun.
Golden moments, freely found,
In vulnerability, love is crowned.

Stars Entwined in the Night

In a canvas of velvet dreams,
Stars like whispers, soft moonbeams.
Radiant dots in endless skies,
Shining bright, old loves arise.

They twinkle secrets, stories told,
Of journeys brave and hearts of gold.
In the dark, they light the way,
Guiding souls in the fray.

Each constellation, a map of fate,
Holding wishes, we contemplate.
Moments captured in cosmic grace,
As time slips by, we find our place.

With each spark, a promise made,
In the silence, dreams cascade.
Boundless beauty, heartbeats synchronize,
In this night, love never dies.

Stars entwined, a dance so pure,
In the vast, we are secure.
Beyond the limits, beyond the night,
In the cosmos, love takes flight.

Sculpting Memories in Time

In the quiet of the night,
Whispers of the past take flight.
Shapes of laughter, etched in air,
Carved in moments, fragile, rare.

Time's embrace holds all we hold,
Stories woven, spun from gold.
Glimmers of joy, echoes of pain,
In the heart, they still remain.

Chiseled dreams in shadows cast,
Reflecting moments, sacred, vast.
Fragments of love, lost and found,
In every heartbeat, they resound.

Each memory a crafted piece,
Holding fragments of our peace.
In the gallery of our mind,
Timeless treasures, intertwined.

So let us mold with gentle hands,
Our lives together, as time expands.
For in each sculpted memory,
Lies the essence of you and me.

The Joy in Little Things

A morning breeze on gentle skin,
The laughter shared, where joys begin.
A warm cup cradled in our hands,
The comfort found in simple plans.

Sunlight dancing on the floor,
The rustle of leaves outside the door.
A moment's peace, a soothing sigh,
Finding beauty in the sky.

A child's smile, pure and bright,
Twinkling stars that grace the night.
The warmth of hugs, the love we bring,
Embracing life's small, precious things.

The sound of rain on windowpanes,
A quiet walk through winding lanes.
In every moment, treasures hide,
In the little things, joy resides.

So let us cherish day by day,
Finding joy in life's ballet.
For in these moments, rich and true,
Lies happiness, just me and you.

Serenity in Shared Silence

In the hush between our words,
A gentle calm, like song of birds.
Eyes meet softly, souls align,
In shared silence, pure and fine.

A peaceful breath, the world fades low,
In this stillness, emotions flow.
Hands entwined, no need for speech,
In silent moments, hearts can reach.

The rustling leaves, a quiet song,
In this space, we both belong.
Time stands still, a breath held tight,
In shared silence, our hearts take flight.

No rush to fill the empty air,
In quietude, we find a prayer.
As whispers of the soul unwind,
In love's embrace, our peace we find.

Let us linger, just you and me,
In serene moments, we are free.
For in silence, bonds are tight,
Embracing love, in gentle light.

Where Two Paths Cross

At the edge of fate's design,
Two paths converge, a twinkling sign.
Journeys meet in unexpected ways,
Blending lives like summer days.

In a glance, a spark ignites,
Shadows dance in fading lights.
Words unspoken, hearts alight,
In this moment, everything feels right.

The stories held within each heart,
A tapestry where lives will start.
Each step together, rich and bold,
Two souls entwined, a tale untold.

The laughter shared, the silent dreams,
In every glance, love redeems.
Where paths converge, new journeys begin,
As life unfolds, our hearts shall win.

So here we stand, on fate's own thread,
Where hopes and dreams, like rivers, spread.
Together bound, forever lost,
In the magic of paths that cross.

The Space Between Our Words

In silence, secrets dwell,
A heartbeat's gentle call,
Emotions left unspoken,
In the void, we feel it all.

A glance, a fleeting thought,
What we dare not share,
In the pauses, worlds are built,
Yet we linger, unaware.

The distance feels like hope,
Between you and my sigh,
In the space between our words,
Love blooms, though we don't try.

Each moment seems profound,
In shadows, light may hide,
The truth lives on the edge,
Where our hearts coincide.

So let us bridge the gap,
With whispers soft and kind,
For in the space between,
Our souls are intertwined.

Finding Fireflies in the Dark

In the twilight's gentle hush,
We wander, hearts alight,
Chasing tiny sparks of joy,
In the velvet cloak of night.

They flicker, dance, and weave,
A symphony of dreams,
Whispers of a magic world,
Where nothing's as it seems.

With every step we take,
A wonder fills the air,
These fleeting jewels of dusk,
Remind us to be fair.

A moment caught in time,
Beneath the starlit sky,
We hold these glowing treasures,
As fireflies flit by.

Let's gather all their light,
And sprinkle it around,
For in the dark we find grace,
In the beauty we have found.

Stories Etched in Time

In the lines of weathered stone,
History whispers low,
Tales of battles fought and won,
Where memories still glow.

Each mark tells of a life,
Of love, of pain, of grace,
In shadows deep and wide,
We find our rightful place.

Echoes from the distant past,
A tapestry unfolds,
Woven in the fabric,
Of the stories that we hold.

Listen closely to the winds,
They carry voices near,
Of those who came before us,
Their laughter and their fear.

So let's immortalize the tales,
Carve them in our soul,
For every story matters,
They are what makes us whole.

A Garden of Many Seasons

In spring, new blooms arise,
With colors bright and bold,
Life awakens, smiles bloom wide,
As stories now unfold.

Summer dances through the leaves,
In the warmth of golden light,
Nature's symphony of joy,
Filling days with pure delight.

Autumn drapes her cloak in hues,
As leaves begin to fall,
A gentle reminder of change,
That seasons heed the call.

Winter wraps the world in white,
With silence, still and deep,
Yet in this hibernation,
Dreams awaken from their sleep.

Through every season's passage,
The garden thrives and grows,
A reflection of our journeys,
In the ebb and flow it shows.

Candlelight Conversations

In the glow of the flickering flame,
Whispers float like velvet dreams.
Eyes meet in the warmth of the night,
Hearts dance with unspoken themes.

Stories woven in amber light,
Laughter sparkles like stars above.
Every moment a treasure held tight,
In the magic of candlelit love.

Secrets shared with shadows near,
Fingers brush, a delicate touch.
All worries fade, lost in the sphere,
This space crafted, we cherish so much.

Time slows down, the world fades away,
Only the flicker and breath remain.
Candlelight embraces the night's play,
In these moments, joy conquers pain.

As the flame dances, so do we,
A rhythm shared, pure and divine.
In candid talks, we're truly free,
Candlelight, our chime, our sign.

Clarity in the Chaos

In the swirl of a stormy mind,
Stillness whispers in every thought.
From the maze of confusion unwind,
Seek the clarity that we've sought.

Amidst the noise, a gentle hum,
Voices converge in a sacred song.
With every beat, senses become,
Stronger; our resolve is lifelong.

Peering through the tempestuous haze,
A single truth begins to shine.
With each breath, the clouds start to graze,
Revealing paths that intertwine.

In the chaos, beauty can bloom,
If we learn to pause and reflect.
Even darkness can bring forth room,
For the light that we all can protect.

Finding peace in the wild unknown,
Together, we navigate the fray.
In our hearts, a strength has grown,
Clarity guides us on our way.

The Threads of Time Woven Together

Golden strands stretch through the air,
Moments that spark like fireflies.
In the tapestry, love and care,
Brush strokes of fate beneath the skies.

Each thread a story yet to tell,
Weaving history's rich embrace.
Through laughter shared and tears fell,
Life's fabric forms a sacred space.

With every twist, fate's gentle hand,
Shapes our journey, each step we take.
From distant shores to grains of sand,
Connections made that never break.

In the loom of existence, stand tall,
Together, we stitch a vast design.
Through trials faced, we rise and fall,
Threads of time, in love, intertwine.

As seasons shift and ages blend,
The past lingers, the future calls.
In this we find, as souls transcend,
Our shared journey breaks down the walls.

The Hidden Language of Affection

In the quiet moments we share,
Words unspoken fill the air.
Glimmers of love cross our gaze,
A language crafted, gentle praise.

A soft touch speaks volumes true,
Fingers entwined, hearts break through.
In laughter's echo, sweet refrains,
Affection blooms like summer rains.

Secret smiles that steal the light,
Whispers linger into the night.
With every gaze, a promise made,
In this dance, our fears do fade.

Between the lines, understanding grows,
In silence, our hearts overflow.
Connection strong, a gentle sway,
In hidden meanings, we find our way.

This language rare, we hold so dear,
A tapestry woven through every year.
In simple gestures, love takes flight,
The hidden language of pure delight.

The Dance of Two Shadows

In twilight's soft embrace, they sway,
Two shadows twirling, lost in play.
Beneath the moon's soft, silver beam,
They dance as one, a whispered dream.

Steps draw near, hearts beat as one,
In the night, their fears undone.
Mirrored moves in gentle grace,
A silent song, time can't erase.

Whispers of the night take flight,
As shadows blend in soft moonlight.
Each curve and turn a tale to tell,
In the dance where echoes dwell.

Bound by fate, they glide and weave,
With every step, they dare believe.
The world retreats, just they remain,
In the shadows, love's refrain.

As dawn breaks with a gentle sigh,
Their shadows linger, yet they fly.
In every dance, a promise found,
In the silence, love's heart sound.

A Symphony in Silence

In the quiet, notes unfold,
A symphony of tales untold.
Whispers linger in the air,
Melodies that speak with care.

Nature hums a gentle tune,
Underneath the watchful moon.
Leaves rustle, a soft ballet,
In this silence, dreams hold sway.

Each pause a breath, a heart's delight,
As stars above ignite the night.
The world around takes on a hue,
In silence, bonds of love renew.

Hidden sounds, like secrets flow,
In every shadow, stories grow.
A rhythm found in tender glances,
In the quiet, love advances.

When words fail, emotions sing,
In silence, every heartbeat's swing.
A language forged beyond time's wall,
In this stillness, we have it all.

When Time Stood Still

In a moment, the world paused bright,
Caught in a dream wrapped in light.
Seconds danced with grace untold,
As echoes of love slowly unfold.

Eyes met, and the clocks forgot,
A timeless bond, a single thought.
The universe, with bated breath,
Held its space as love danced with death.

The shadows faded, yet they stayed,
In this sweet stillness, emotions played.
With every heartbeat, the world aligned,
In the silence, their souls entwined.

Hours passed, yet none could feel,
In that instant, everything real.
Memories forged in fleeting grace,
When time stood still, they found their place.

As life resumed with a gentle sigh,
They cherished the moment, you and I.
In every tick, a heartbeat's thrill,
Together in love, when time stood still.

The Art of Togetherness

In every glance, a thought expressed,
In shared silence, we find our rest.
Together we weave a tapestry bright,
In the folds of love, endless light.

Steps in sync as we walk the way,
Hand in hand, come what may.
Painting moments in vibrant tones,
The art of togetherness calls us home.

Laughter echoes in playful sound,
In each shared joy, our souls are found.
With dreams entwined, we build our nest,
In harmony's embrace, we are blessed.

Days unfold like petals, soft and sweet,
In this journey, our hearts compete.
With each sunrise, fresh hopes appear,
The art of togetherness, crystal clear.

As seasons change and time flows on,
With every dusk, a new dawn drawn.
In this canvas of life, side by side,
The art of love, our truest pride.

Whispers in the Workshop

In the glow of the lantern's light,
Tools lay scattered with delight.
Each hammer's strike a song to sing,
Carved from wood, the dreams take wing.

Dust motes dance in silence true,
Creating visions, old and new.
Whispers echo, hands at play,
Crafting time, day by day.

A chisel's edge, a gentle touch,
Life in timber, oh so much.
Every grain tells tales of yore,
In this workshop, we explore.

Hearts beat strong with hopeful sound,
In each creation, love is found.
A legacy of craft and care,
In the workshop, spirits share.

So let the wood and metal blend,
In this space, our dreams ascend.
Together, we shape, we define,
Whispers sing, our hearts align.

Unseen Fortunes of Devotion

In quiet corners, love resides,
Unseen treasures where hope abides.
A gentle touch, a knowing glance,
In devotion's dance, we take our chance.

Each moment shared, a hidden gem,
In whispered words, we find our stem.
In laughter's echo, joy will bloom,
In silent nights, we find our room.

Through storms we sail, hand in hand,
In the depths of love, we stand.
For unseen fortunes often thrive,
In every heartbeat, we feel alive.

With every promise, softly spoken,
The bonds we forge shall ne'er be broken.
A tapestry of hearts entwined,
In whispered vows, pure love defined.

So cherish the bonds we weave each day,
In unseen fortunes, we shall stay.
With devotion's light as our guide,
Together we'll forever abide.

The Art of Unspoken Promises

In a gaze that lingers long,
Lies the truth, raw and strong.
Not always need we say the words,
In silence, love's song is heard.

Promises hang in the quiet air,
Entwined souls that truly care.
A simple touch, a gentle smile,
In that moment, we reconcile.

Through trials faced, through shadows cast,
A bond formed, steadfast and vast.
In trust we find the unvoiced grace,
A sacred space time can't erase.

In the rhythm of breaths combined,
Assured connections, souls aligned.
The art we build without a sound,
In unspoken love, we're forever bound.

So let us weave these threads of fate,
In every heartbeat, we create.
For in the silence, we shall see,
The art of promises, you and me.

Together We Build

With every brick, we lay the base,
In unity, we find our place.
Through laughter shared and dreams combined,
Together we build, hearts aligned.

In storms that test our very will,
We gather strength, we climb the hill.
Hands joined tight, we face the sun,
In this journey, we are one.

With visions bright and hopes held high,
We reach for stars that paint the sky.
Each step we take, each path we tread,
In togetherness, our fears are shed.

In the tapestry of life we weave,
The threads of love we shall believe.
With every laugh, with every cry,
Together, we rise, we soar, we fly.

So here's to dreams that we unfold,
In this life, together, bold.
With every moment that we share,
Together we build, with love and care.

The Weight of Unspoken Promises

Silent words hang heavy in the air,
Each unsaid thought, a weight we bear.
In shadows deep, our hearts reside,
In the quiet night, we cannot hide.

Dreams once whispered fade away,
Lost in time, they drift and sway.
Promises linger, unfulfilled,
In the silence, hope distilled.

Eyes avert, we dare not speak,
The truth we share feels far too bleak.
Yet in the dark, a spark ignites,
Reviving faith on sleepless nights.

Fingers crossed, we tread the dusk,
In doubt we drown, in love we trust.
Each promise lingers, an echo's sigh,
Beneath the stars, we wonder why.

Through the void, a whisper calls,
In our hearts, the silence falls.
For unspoken words can still convey,
A love that grows in shadows, day by day.

Gardener of Hearts

In a world of blooms, you gently tread,
Tending to flowers, where dreams are fed.
With tender care, you plant the seeds,
Watering hopes and nurturing needs.

Through storms that rage and skies of grey,
You persevere, come what may.
With every touch, you heal the ground,
In your embrace, lost souls are found.

Sunlight dances on petals bright,
In your presence, darkness takes flight.
You cultivate love with every breath,
Transforming loss into paths of depth.

In whispers soft, you sow the grace,
A touch of kindness in every space.
Through laughter shared and tears that fall,
You're the gardener tending us all.

So here's to you, with hands so true,
In the garden where love blooms anew.
Your heart of gold, a beacon of light,
Guiding us through the endless night.

Echoes in an Empty Room

In corners where silence softly creeps,
Shadows linger, where memory sleeps.
Each whispering sigh, a timeless trace,
In an empty room, you find your place.

The walls remember laughter and tears,
Ghosts of the past still linger near.
With every heartbeat, a story told,
In the stillness, emotions unfold.

Sunbeams break through the dusty glass,
Playing like ghosts of moments past.
Each echo bounces, soft and low,
Haunting the heart with what we know.

Though space is bare, it holds the weight,
Of promises made and love's cruel fate.
In shadows deep, our souls align,
In an empty room, your heart's still mine.

So let the echoes speak for us,
In the quiet, we still trust.
For in these walls, where time stands still,
Love lingers on, and always will.

Threads of Longing

With each thread pulled, we weave our dreams,
Stitching together our silent screams.
In the fabric of time, longing weaves,
A tapestry rich with hopes and leaves.

Shadows dance in the fading light,
Between the stitches, I grasp your sight.
Every loop holds a heartbeat near,
In the threads of longing, you are here.

Like a quilt that warms a wintry night,
You wrap my soul in the softest light.
Though distance stretches between the lines,
In every knot, our fate entwines.

The colors blend where heartaches meet,
Creating patterns both bitter and sweet.
Through woven paths, together we roam,
In the threads of longing, you've become home.

So I'll keep sewing through night and day,
With every thread, I'll find a way.
As long as fibers of hope remain,
In this tapestry, love will sustain.

Weaving Our Story

In threads of gold, we stitch our past,
Moments captured, memories cast.
Through laughter's glow and tears that fall,
We weave our story, a tapestry tall.

With each new day, a pattern unfolds,
Stories of courage, waiting to be told.
In the fabric of life, we find our place,
Each strand a tale, each thread a grace.

Together we gather, hands intertwined,
In the loom of time, our lives aligned.
For every joy, for every sigh,
We weave a legacy that will not die.

In shared moments, our hearts collide,
A tapestry rich, where love does abide.
Through trials and triumphs, we carry on,
In the art of living, forever drawn.

Our story unravels, yet never in vain,
Through storms and sunshine, through laughter and pain.
In the weave of our journey, forever we find,
The beauty in moments, two souls intertwined.

Together in the Struggle

With weary hands, we face the tide,
In battles fought, we stand side by side.
Each challenge met, a step we tread,
Together in struggle, where hope is bred.

The weight is heavy, the journey long,
Yet in our hearts, we find the song.
With every loss, we rise anew,
Together we gather, our strength in view.

Through stormy nights and sunlit days,
We carve a path, in myriad ways.
In each scar earned, and dream we chase,
Together we thrive, in this boundless space.

The hurdles test us, but we don't break,
In unity's arms, we learn to awake.
With hearts unyielding, we march along,
Together in struggle, we craft our song.

For the bonds forged in trials now shine,
In every heartbeat, our spirits align.
With hands held tight, we journey as one,
Together in struggle, until new dawns begun.

The Embrace of Effort

In early dawn, we rise with dreams,
The path ahead, a flow of streams.
In every effort, we sow the seeds,
The embrace of labor, our spirit feeds.

With steady hands, we shape the clay,
In passion's fire, we find our way.
Through sweat and toil, our hopes ignite,
In the embrace of effort, we find the light.

Each heartbeat echoes, the rhythm of fight,
In shadows deep, we search for sight.
Together we climb, through valleys low,
The embrace of effort, where courage grows.

With every stumble, we learn to rise,
In the struggle, our strength belies.
With eyes on the summit, we push through the strife,
The embrace of effort, the essence of life.

As stars align, our dreams will blend,
In this journey together, there's no end.
Through effort and hope, our hearts will soar,
The embrace of effort opens every door.

Woven Paths of Kinship

In gentle whispers, our tales entwine,
Woven paths of kinship, forever we shine.
In laughter shared, in sorrow's depth,
We find our way, each breath a gift.

Through seasons changing, we stand so near,
In threads of love, we conquer fear.
With open hearts, we welcome the dawn,
Woven paths of kinship, forever drawn.

In every embrace, a story is told,
In warmth of friendship, we brave the cold.
With every tear, a bond will grow,
Woven paths of kinship, a vibrant glow.

Through challenges faced, we lift each other,
In the fabric of trust, we're woven like a mother.
Through trials endured, and joys expressed,
Woven paths of kinship, we are blessed.

So here we stand, come what may,
In woven paths, we boldly stay.
For in unity's power, we find our way,
Woven paths of kinship, forever we play.

The Blueprint of Companionship

In the quiet hum of dawn,
Two hearts sketch a simple plan.
Paths entwined like whispered dreams,
Drawing lines, intricate seams.

Hand in hand, we trace our way,
Through shadows where the young hearts play.
With laughter woven, soft and bright,
We build our world, a canvas light.

A cornerstone of trust is laid,
In every choice that we have made.
Foundations strong, through storms we stand,
Creating joy, a guiding hand.

In moments shared, we shape our lore,
Crafting tales forevermore.
Each glance a brushstroke, each smile a hue,
Together, we paint our vision true.

With every season, we grow and change,
Yet still remain, fond and strange.
An everlasting bond defined,
A blueprint love, forever signed.

In the Lantern's Glow

Beneath the stars, we whisper low,
In the soft warmth of lantern's glow.
Shadows dance in the hushed night air,
Glimmers of secrets, we happily share.

The world fades, becomes a dream,
In this moment, life feels supreme.
With candlelight flickers, laughter ignites,
Filling our hearts, igniting delights.

As time slips softly, we linger near,
Counting each heartbeat, drawing you near.
In the amber glow, our worries cease,
Wrapped in comfort, we find our peace.

Unveiling stories under the moon,
A melody sweet, a whispered tune.
Two souls entwined in the twilight haze,
Lost in love's soft, enchanting gaze.

With every flicker, dreams we sow,
Our lantern glows, forever aglow.
Together we cherish, together we grow,
In the warmth of our love, ever so slow.

A Tapestry of Quiet Moments

In the stillness, we find our art,
Threads of silence stitch the heart.
Gentle whispers weave between,
A tapestry soft, yet unseen.

With each sunrise, new colors blend,
Harmony grows, our spirits mend.
Simple gestures, a shared glance,
Creating rhythm, a tranquil dance.

Amidst the chaos, we carve our time,
Unearthing treasures, unspoken rhyme.
Moments linger, like pages turned,
In every heartbeat, love is learned.

Laughter echoes in quiet places,
Memory's warmth, our sacred spaces.
Fading sunlight, a soft embrace,
In every shuffle, a tender trace.

As days meld into nights that bloom,
We stitch our dreams in this sweet room.
Time stands still; the world can wait,
In quiet moments, we celebrate.

Unfolding Stories of Us

Like petals soft, we gently unfold,
Tales of love and of dreams told.
Each chapter new, like whispered grace,
In our hearts, we carve a place.

Through valleys deep and mountains high,
We share the tears, we share the sigh.
In laughter's light, our spirits soar,
Every moment a chance for more.

Unfurling like pages in a book,
Choosing love for every look.
In the silence, our stories breathe,
Crafting paths, the heart bequeath.

With ink of hope, we write the lines,
Bound together, our fate entwines.
Each verse a promise, soft and true,
In the story of me, there's always you.

The tales we share never grow old,
In every heartbeat, our lives retold.
With every sunrise, new tales begin,
Unfolding stories, our love within.

The Harmony of Handwritten Letters

In ink and paper, thoughts take flight,
A dance of words, both soft and bright.
Each curve and line, a story spun,
In quiet whispers, hearts are won.

With every stroke, a tale unfolds,
Secrets shared, and feelings bold.
The rhythm flows, a soulful song,
In letters penned, we all belong.

The scent of parchment, memories cling,
A treasure trove of what we bring.
Echoes linger, moments trace,
In handwritten notes, we find our place.

Embracing flaws, imperfections show,
Each letter speaks, as feelings grow.
A timeless bond, through words we weave,
In harmony, we dare believe.

So cherish each line, every verse,
In these small gestures, we immerse.
For in the art of calligraphy,
Lies the essence of our unity.

Labouring for Each Other

In fields of toil, we stand as one,
With outstretched hands, our work begun.
Together we lift, together we strive,
In shared endeavors, we come alive.

Each burden carried, our spirits entwined,
In sacrifice, true love we find.
Through sweat and tears, we pave the way,
For brighter tomorrows, come what may.

From dawn till dusk, we build and mend,
In unity's name, our hearts defend.
We labor not for self, but more,
For those beside us, whom we adore.

In quiet moments, gratitude sings,
For all the joy that giving brings.
Hand in hand, through thick and thin,
We find our strength, our voices win.

So let us toil, let our hands be strong,
For in this struggle, we all belong.
In the tapestry of life, we see,
The beauty born from unity.

The Fire that Warms

A flicker glows in the velvet night,
Embers dance with warmth and light.
Around the hearth, we gather near,
In the fire's glow, we draw our cheer.

Stories shared in the crackling sound,
Laughter and memories all around.
The heat that pulses, hearts embrace,
In the fire's arms, we find our place.

Each flame a spirit, bright and bold,
Illuminating secrets untold.
In the flickers, our hopes ignite,
A beacon guiding through the night.

With every spark, the past revives,
A testament to our lives.
In this warmth, we are reborn,
From weary trials, our strength is worn.

So let the fire dance and sway,
As we share our dreams at the end of the day.
In its embrace, we find our way,
The fire that warms, come what may.

Weaving Dreams into Reality

Threads of wishes, colors bright,
Weaving visions into the light.
With hands of hope, we stitch the seams,
Crafting futures from our dreams.

Each knot and loop, a tale we tell,
In the fabric of life, we weave so well.
From every doubt, a pattern grows,
In the tapestry of what we chose.

Patience needed, as we create,
With every stitch, we celebrate.
Together we work, hand in hand,
In this shared journey, we take a stand.

Inspiration flows, a river wide,
Through hopes and fears, we will abide.
With every thread, we make it real,
In the art of weaving, we feel.

So gather your dreams and share them here,
For in this circle, we draw near.
Together we'll craft the life we seek,
Weaving dreams into reality, unique.

Dancing Between the Minutes

In the hush of fleeting time,
We sway to whispers soft and sweet.
Each second holds a secret rhyme,
In the rhythm, our hearts meet.

Ink black skies, a twinkling glow,
Stars twirl like dreams in tender flight.
With every step, the shadows grow,
In this dance, we find the light.

Lost in moments, smiles collide,
Eyes sparkle with a tender glance.
Our spirits lift, our fears subside,
Together, we embrace the chance.

Beats of laughter paint the air,
As joy ignites the silent night.
Together, we shed every care,
In the dance that feels so right.

When the hourglass runs its course,
We'll treasure each precious swirl.
In the ballet of love's force,
We find our place in this world.

The Craft of Intimacy

In quiet moments, hands entwined,
Our hearts speak words too deep for sound.
With gentle touches, love defined,
In this magic, we are found.

Every glance holds worlds unknown,
A canvas brushed with vibrant hues.
In the silence, seeds are sown,
An art where love's the only muse.

Lost in layers, depths unfold,
Each story woven, thread by thread.
In closeness, all our truths are told,
In every heartbeat, hopes are fed.

With whispers soft, we build our space,
A sanctuary, warm and near.
In love's embrace, we find our place,
Where all our doubts just disappear.

Together, we craft each embrace,
A timeless dance of trust and care.
In the art of love, we find grace,
In the moments that we share.

In the Shadows of Togetherness

In shadows cast by twilight's hue,
We find a warmth that stirs the night.
With hands of love, we craft anew,
A world where everything feels right.

The moonlight bathes our whispered fears,
While laughter dances on the breeze.
Here in the dark, love's light appears,
A shelter formed with perfect ease.

Through storms of doubt and fleeting time,
We build a shelter, strong and true.
In every breath, a shared rhyme,
In every glance, a promise too.

In quiet moments, souls ignite,
As shadows blend, we feel the spark.
Together, we rise, out of spite,
Finding our way within the dark.

The beauty lies in what we share,
Each heartbeat echoes stories told.
In the shadows, love's warmth is rare,
A treasure more precious than gold.

Voices of Understanding

In the gentle hum of life around,
We hear the song of hearts so true.
With every word and silence found,
There lies a bridge that lights the blue.

Each voice a note in harmony,
Resonates with echoes of care.
The melodies that set us free,
In shared stories, burdens bear.

Through trials faced and joy embraced,
We gather pieces, lost and found.
In the tapestry, love is laced,
With threads of understanding sound.

Together we weave our truth,
Each heartbeat pulses with intent.
In youthful hopes and softened ruth,
Our minds align, our spirits vent.

As voices merge in timeless song,
We find the strength to rise above.
In this chorus, we belong,
Through every note, we breathe in love.

The Healing of Fractured Hearts

In shadows cast by silent tears,
A whisper calls, it draws us near.
With gentle hands, we start to mend,
Two broken souls begin to blend.

Through time and trust, the wounds will fade,
A tender light in love displayed.
Each heartbeat sings a soft refrain,
Of hopes renewed, despite the pain.

As cracked facades find strength anew,
In every scar, a story true.
The journey holds both joy and strife,
Yet love will chart the course of life.

Embracing flaws, we rise and stand,
A symphony, hand in hand.
With open hearts, we learn to feel,
In fractured parts, the strength to heal.

So here we stand, in love's embrace,
United close, a sacred space.
With every heartbeat, our souls ignite,
Two fractured hearts in the soft twilight.

Beneath the Stars' Shared Secrets

Underneath the velvet night,
Stars above, they shine so bright.
Whispers dance on gentle breeze,
Secrets shared among the trees.

Each twinkle holds a tale untold,
Of dreams and hopes, both brave and bold.
In cosmic light, we find our way,
Guided by the moon's soft sway.

With every glance, a story flows,
In silent words, our heartstrings grow.
Beneath the stars, two souls take flight,
In magic's grip, we lose the night.

In this vast space, we dare to dream,
With love so pure, we're lost, it seems.
A universe of hearts entwined,
In starlit paths, our fate designed.

So let us wander 'neath the sky,
With whispered prayers that never die.
Each star a promise, a spark, a chance,
Beneath the heavens, our hearts will dance.

The Map of My Heartbeat

A compass drawn in softest ink,
Marks every joy, the tears we think.
With every pulse, a journey starts,
The map unfolds, it charts our hearts.

Through valleys deep and mountains high,
With every step, we learn to fly.
In sacred paths, we find our way,
The heart's true rhythm leads the play.

Each beat a whisper, soft but clear,
A melody only love can hear.
With every mark, a tale of old,
Of warmth and light, of courage bold.

In moments shared, our voices rise,
Creating worlds beneath the skies.
The map we hold connects us tight,
In union's glow, we find our light.

So follow where this journey leads,
In every pulse, love plants its seeds.
A lasting bond, forever beet,
Together drawn, the map of heartbeat.

Glistening in the Daylight

When morning rays awaken dreams,
The world ignites with golden beams.
Each dewdrop glistens, fresh and new,
A canvas bright with skies of blue.

In laughter shared and smiles so wide,
We bask in warmth, our hearts collide.
With every moment, time stands still,
In daylight's glow, we find our will.

Nature's brush paints colors bold,
In every hue, our stories told.
The sun ignites our spirits free,
In this embrace, we simply be.

As shadows dance and softly sway,
Life's radiant pulse guides our way.
Glistening paths beneath our feet,
In daylight's arms, our souls compete.

So let us cherish each sunrise,
With grateful hearts and open eyes.
For in this light, we find our song,
Glistening bright, where we belong.

Chasing Shadows of Longing

In the twilight's gentle glow,
Whispers of dreams begin to flow.
Echoes of laughter in the night,
Faint memories lost from sight.

Footsteps on paths once walked,
Silent words, unspoken talk.
Hearts ache for what cannot be,
Chasing shadows, longing free.

Moonlight dances on the trees,
Carried softly on the breeze.
Fleeting moments, grasp them tight,
As they vanish, out of sight.

Each sigh builds a fragile thread,
Life's fabric woven, hopes we tread.
Finding solace in the pain,
Chasing shadows once again.

Though the dawn will break our trance,
We hold onto the fleeting chance.
In the chase, we find our song,
Chasing shadows, we belong.

Bonds Forged in Fire

In the furnace of our might,
We emerge, ignited bright.
Passion fuels the flames we hold,
In unity, our story's told.

Through trials that shape our soul,
Each challenge makes us whole.
Hand in hand, we face the storm,
Together, we transform.

Molten dreams, a vision clear,
In the heat, we shed our fear.
Steel and spirit intertwine,
Forged in fire, hearts align.

We rise from ashes, bold and true,
Bonds unbroken, tried and new.
With every spark, a brighter fate,
In the fire, love won't wait.

As embers cool and shadows grow,
We stand strong, a fierce glow.
In the warmth, our souls inspire,
Together, bonds forged in fire.

The Melody of Unison

In the hush of the twilight air,
Voices blend, a song to share.
Each note strikes a chord so pure,
In unison, hearts endure.

Harmony weaves through the night,
Creating beauty, pure delight.
Together we sing, hand in hand,
A melody, a timeless band.

Rhythms pulse beneath our skin,
A dance where we all begin.
With every sound, our spirits rise,
In this symphony, love amplifies.

The silence fades, replaced by grace,
As we find our rightful place.
Each voice contributes to the tune,
Under the watch of a silver moon.

In every heartbeat, every sigh,
We weave a tale that won't die.
Together, we find our bliss,
The melody, a sacred kiss.

Crafting Harmony in Chaos

In the storm where shadows play,
We find our strength in disarray.
Chaos swirls like distant thunder,
Yet we rise, our hearts in wonder.

With every clash, we mold the sound,
From discord, beauty can be found.
Fragments of life in wild array,
Crafting harmony, come what may.

Voices blend in vibrant hue,
Painting calm where once was blue.
Together we build, piece by piece,
In this chaos, we find peace.

A dance of hearts, a weaving thread,
Each moment cherished, lovingly spread.
Through the noise, our spirits soar,
Crafting harmony forevermore.

In the end, we find our way,
Together, come what may.
Through the chaos, bright and clear,
Crafting harmony, we draw near.

The Ties that Bind Us

In every laugh, a bond is formed,
In every tear, our hearts are warmed.
Through stormy nights and sunny days,
Together we navigate life's maze.

With whispered dreams and shared hopes,
We find strength in simple scopes.
Hand in hand, we face the tide,
In unity, we take our stride.

Though distance may stretch like the sea,
In our hearts, we carry the key.
The threads of love weave and entwine,
In every heartbeat, you are mine.

With every step, our story grows,
In laughter's echo, affection flows.
Through silent moments and loud cheer,
Together always, we persevere.

In twilight's glow, we share our fears,
In every joy, we shed our tears.
Bound by the ties that time can't sever,
In this journey, we are forever.

A Side by Side Journey

Through winding paths, we tread so near,
With every step, we hold what's dear.
In shadows cast by setting sun,
Our laughter rings, our hearts are one.

With every hill, a story told,
In whispers soft, our dreams unfold.
We share the weight of heavy loads,
In solemn vows and secret codes.

As morning light breaks fresh and bright,
We find our way, hearts full of light.
Side by side, we chase the dawn,
On this path, we're never withdrawn.

The journey stretches, yet we grow,
With every step, together we sow.
In fields of gold and skies of blue,
Each moment shared feels fresh and new.

Through twists and turns, we won't lose sight,
In darkest hours, we bring the light.
With every mile, we build our tale,
Side by side, we'll never fail.

Threads of Connection

In quiet moments, we intertwine,
Threads of warmth in designs divine.
With every smile, a tapestry spun,
In the weave of love, we are one.

Through laughter's glow and sorrow's weight,
Our lives connect, it's truly fate.
Each thread a tale, each knot a sign,
In this fabric, your heart is mine.

Though storms may shake the fibers tight,
Together, we bring the calm and light.
In every stitch, our hopes align,
Crafting dreams in perfect design.

The colors blend, they shimmer bright,
Illuminating our shared plight.
In every tear, a new thread shows,
Binding us close as life flows.

The roots we plant, the seeds we sow,
Grow stronger through the ebb and flow.
In this journey, hand in hand we roam,
In these threads, we've found our home.

Within the Shared Space

In quiet corners where we meet,
The world outside fades to a beat.
Within this space, our laughter sings,
Creating joy from simple things.

Each glance exchanged, a story told,
Within these walls, our hearts unfold.
In whispered dreams and shared delight,
Together, we embrace the night.

Through every silence, there's a thread,
In unspoken words, our spirits spread.
Within this bond, we find our way,
Guiding each other, day by day.

With every heartbeat, time moves slow,
In this shared space, our love can grow.
Through every challenge, we stand tall,
Together we rise, never to fall.

As seasons change and years unfold,
The memories crafted are pure gold.
Within this space, forever may dwell,
In the magic of us, all is well.

Beneath the Surface of Us

In whispered tones, we share our dreams,
A world unseen, where magic gleams.
With every glance, a story grows,
Beneath the skin, a river flows.

In shadows cast, our truths reside,
The pulsing beat of hearts allied.
With every sigh, we bridge the space,
An ocean deep, we intertwine in grace.

In silence, we uncover fears,
The weight of past and future years.
Yet, hand in hand, we face the night,
Our souls ignited, pure and bright.

Beneath the surface, love ignites,
A spark of hope in darkest nights.
Together, woven, side by side,
In every tear, in every tide.

As time unfurls, we find our way,
In tangled roots, where shadows play.
Through every storm, we rise anew,
In depths profound, it's me and you.

Threads of Destiny Weave

In the tapestry of stars that shine,
Threads of fate intertwine, divine.
With every whisper, destiny calls,
In gentle patterns, the universe sprawls.

Each woven strand, a life to live,
Moments shared, the love we give.
In cosmic dance, our spirits flow,
Bound by the threads of what we know.

Through time's embrace, we journey far,
Connected by the same guiding star.
In every heartbeat, a silent vow,
Together, in the here and now.

In the loom of life, we find our place,
Stitched with laughter, stitched with grace.
From heart to heart, our stories thread,
In vibrant colors, our dreams are spread.

Though twists may come, and paths may sway,
United, we shape our own ballet.
In the dance of fate, we find our way,
Threads of destiny, forever stay.

The Alchemy of Hearts

In the crucible of quiet flames,
We blend our hopes, we forge our names.
With every touch, a spark ignites,
Transforming shadows into lights.

In whispered secrets, potions brew,
The essence of love, pure and true.
From sorrow's dust, we craft our gold,
In ancient tales, our lives unfold.

With alchemical power, we unite,
In hopeful visions, soaring heights.
Two souls entwined, a single beat,
In sacred circles, we find our heat.

Through trials faced, our bond refines,
In the alchemy of hearts, love shines.
With every moment, we dare to dream,
In the potion of life, our spirits teem.

In magic's glow, we dance again,
As pendant stars weave through the zen.
In every heartbeat, the world ignites,
In the alchemy of love, we take flight.

Quiet Echoes of an Endless Dance

In twilight's hush, our shadows blend,
A silent rhythm, where time transcends.
With every step, the music plays,
In quiet echoes, through endless days.

Beneath the stars, we sway and glide,
In perfect harmony, side by side.
The world fades away, a soft romance,
As whispers weave through our gentle dance.

With every turn, we lose our fears,
In the stillness, our laughter clears.
In moments shared, we find our song,
Together, where we both belong.

Through dusk till dawn, the fire glows,
In silent vows, our friendship grows.
In quiet echoes, our hearts align,
In endless dance, you are forever mine.

As shadows stretch and daylight breaks,
In every heartbeat, our love awakes.
In timeless steps, we forge a trance,
In quiet echoes, an endless dance.

Surrender to the Embrace

In the quiet nights, we find our peace,
Wrapped in warmth, our worries cease.
Soft whispers dance, like shadows sway,
In tender arms, we drift away.

Stars above us, a guiding light,
With every heartbeat, we ignite.
Lost in a world where time stands still,
Surrendering to love's sweet thrill.

The gentle breeze carries our sighs,
In this embrace, our spirits rise.
Beneath the moon, dreams start to weave,
In this cocoon, we learn to believe.

Every breath shared, a promise made,
In each other's eyes, our fears fade.
With every heartbeat, we intertwine,
Two souls in sync, a line divine.

As dawn breaks softly, the shadows retreat,
In this embrace, our hearts repeat.
Together we stand, unafraid to show,
In surrendering here, we continue to grow.

The Map of Us

On parchment worn, we trace the lines,
Mapping moments, your hand in mine.
Each corner turned, a memory made,
In this journey, our love won't fade.

Through valleys low and mountains tall,
Together we rise, together we fall.
In laughter shared and tears misplaced,
We write our story, time can't erase.

X marks the spot of our first kiss,
A treasure found in moments of bliss.
With every route, our hearts align,
In the map of us, your love is mine.

Navigating through life's wild maze,
In every challenge, our spirits blaze.
Side by side, we'll carve our way,
Through storms and sun, come what may.

As stories unfold on this canvas vast,
In every laugh, in every cast.
Together we forge our love so true,
In the map of us, it's me and you.

Chasing Fleeting Glances

In crowded rooms, our eyes collide,
A fleeting moment, a secret ride.
With every glance, a spark ignites,
Silent conversations in whispered nights.

Through the noise, a calm we find,
In stolen peeks, our hearts entwined.
A blush, a smile, a playful tease,
In subtle gestures, we find our ease.

The world around us seems to fade,
In these encounters, our fears evade.
Chasing shadows, we weave our tale,
In this dance, we shall prevail.

Each glance a promise, a wish unfurled,
In these moments, we find our world.
With every shift, anticipation grows,
In fleeting glances, our love flows.

As day turns to night, the magic stays,
In captured moments, in countless ways.
A journey begun with eyes that meet,
In chasing glances, our hearts repeat.

Sculpting Dreams with Touch

With gentle hands, we mold the clay,
Sculpting dreams in a vivid array.
Fingers dancing, creating anew,
In every shape, a vision true.

The warmth of your touch ignites the fire,
In our creation, we find desire.
Through textures soft and forms so grand,
Together we shape our wonderland.

Each stroke whispers tales untold,
In the space between, our hearts unfold.
With passion strong, we carve our fate,
In this art, we celebrate.

As colors blend, the masterpiece grows,
In every contour, our love glows.
With every touch, our souls collide,
In sculpting dreams, we're redefined.

We shape the world with hopes so bright,
In our creation, we find the light.
Together we mold, forever attach,
In sculpting dreams with every touch.

Heartbeats in Sync

In the quiet moments, we find our way,
A rhythm unbroken, come what may.
Your heart whispers softly, a tender call,
Together we rise, we will not fall.

With every heartbeat, a promise made,
In shadows and light, our fears shall fade.
We dance to the sound of love's embrace,
Two souls entwined in a sacred space.

Through storms that may come, we'll stand so strong,
In the harmony of us, where we belong.
Like stars that align in the vast night sky,
Together, forever, just you and I.

In the silence shared, our dreams take flight,
We hold each other, a beacon of light.
With hope in our hearts, we'll venture forth,
In the symphony of life, you are my north.

This journey we travel, hand in hand,
With every heartbeat, we understand.
Love is the rhythm, ever true,
In heartbeats in sync, I'll always choose you.

Building Tomorrow Together

With dreams like bricks, we lay the ground,
In spaces shared, hopes abound.
Each small gesture builds our trust,
In the future's light, we can't combust.

A vision of tomorrow, bright and clear,
We face the challenges without fear.
Through laughter and tears, we find the way,
In the blueprint of life, together we'll stay.

As seasons shift and time unfolds,
In every story, our love is told.
With hands entwined, we shape the day,
In building tomorrow, we find our way.

The dreams we craft are strong and bold,
In the tapestry of life, our colors unfold.
Each challenge faced makes us grow,
In unity, together we flow.

From the ashes of doubt, we rise and soar,
With every heartbeat, we build much more.
In the journey ahead, side by side,
Together we'll thrive, with love as our guide.

The Gentle Art of Care

In tender moments, we share our light,
A gentle touch, everything feels right.
With eyes that listen and hearts that know,
In the quiet grace, our love will grow.

Through the ups and downs, we find our way,
With whispers of kindness, come what may.
In every gesture, the warmth we spread,
In the art of caring, love is bred.

A simple smile, a knowing glance,
In our journey together, we take the chance.
With patience and trust, we weather the storm,
In the gentle art, our hearts stay warm.

As seasons change and years run deep,
In our shared moments, memories we keep.
With hands that nurture, we build and repair,
In every heartbeat, the gentle art of care.

So let us cherish the little things,
In laughter and joy, our spirit sings.
In this dance of life, let love be the share,
In the gentle art, we always care.

Harvesting Togetherness

In fields of gold beneath the sun,
We gather joy, our hearts as one.
With every seed sown, a bond we weave,
In the bounty of life, we choose to believe.

Through hands in soil, we shape our fate,
In laughter shared, we cultivate.
From every moment, richness flows,
In the garden of life, together it grows.

With morning light, our spirits rise,
In shared endeavors, the world is wise.
With every harvest, we find our place,
In the embrace of nature, we find grace.

As seasons change and cycles repeat,
In the rhythm of life, our hearts beat.
With gratitude deep, we stand as one,
In harvesting togetherness, our work is done.

With joy in our hearts, we share the feast,
From dawn till dusk, our bonds increased.
In every laugh and every tear,
In the harvest of life, we draw near.

Soulprints on a Dusty Road

Footsteps linger in the sand,
Stories written by the hand.
Each mark a tale, a silent plea,
In the dust, we wander free.

Sunsets blaze with hues of gold,
Memories shared, tales retold.
With every stride, the past we trace,
Find solace in this sacred space.

Winds whisper secrets of the day,
Nature's tune begins to play.
Each stone a witness, strong and bold,
Guiding paths in twilight's fold.

In the silence, truth unfolds,
Lessons learned, the heart beholds.
Soulprints echo, never fade,
On this road, our dreams cascaded.

Through time and dust, we journey on,
Beneath the stars, at the break of dawn.
Though miles may part what once was near,
Soulprints linger, ever clear.

The Color of Our Conversations

Whispers weave a vibrant thread,
In the air where words are spread.
Crimson laughter, azure dreams,
Conversations burst at the seams.

Soft hues dance in evening light,
Every heartbeat, pure delight.
Emerald hopes and amber sighs,
In every glance, a world that lies.

Shadows blend with shades of gold,
Every story gently told.
In the silence, colors bloom,
Painting life with vivid room.

Cobalt thoughts swirl in the night,
Echoes shimmer, pure and bright.
Together we craft a vibrant brew,
In these moments, me and you.

Each word a stroke, a brush divine,
Creating art in space and time.
The palette rich, our canvas vast,
In the dance of color, we hold fast.

Moments of Stillness

In the hush of the early morn,
Nature's breath is softly born.
A pause in time, the world stands still,
Moments taken, hearts to fill.

Gentle ripples on a glassy lake,
Each reflection, a chance to wake.
A sigh of peace, the calm arrives,
In stillness, we feel alive.

Clouds float by on whispering winds,
In silence, the soul rescinds.
With every heartbeat, echoes blend,
Moments of joy that never end.

Time slows down, a fleeting chance,
To breathe and feel, to dream and dance.
In twilight's glow, we find our way,
Moments of stillness lead the day.

As shadows fade and stars emerge,
In quietness, life will surge.
These moments brief, forever stay,
In our hearts, they find their way.

Whispers of Yesterday

Faint echoes in the evening glow,
Stories carried by winds that blow.
Memories linger, soft and clear,
Whispers of yesterday, we hold dear.

A tapestry of laughter shared,
In the fabric of time, we are bared.
Fleeting glimpses of days gone by,
In every moment, we still fly.

Golden rays touch the faded past,
In the heart, their warmth will last.
In shadows cast by moonlit skies,
Whispers of love that never dies.

Through the corridors of our minds,
Time unfolds and gently binds.
Each memory a thread we weave,
In whispers sweet, we believe.

With every heartbeat, they return,
In silence, nostalgic fires burn.
Embracing fragments, we remain,
Whispers of yesterday, our sweet refrain.

Fragments of a Shared Whisper

In the quiet night we speak,
Words like stars begin to leak.
Echoes dance in soft moonlight,
Whispers weave, unseen, in flight.

Memory holds the tender trace,
Of laughter shared, a warm embrace.
Through the gaps, our voices blend,
A symphony that has no end.

Each shared glance, a silent plea,
A bond formed where hearts can be.
Fleeting moments stitched with care,
Closer still, we linger there.

In dreams we wander, side by side,
Through paths where light and shadow bide.
Fragments dance like dreams in flight,
Together shining, pure delight.

In the silence, we reside,
With every whisper, worlds collide.
Our stories stitched with silver thread,
In whispered dreams, our hearts are fed.

Mosaic of Our Moments

Colors blend in vibrant hues,
Every piece, a tale to choose.
Fragments of laughter, joy and tears,
Together built across the years.

In shadows cast and sunlight bright,
Our memories dance, a joyful sight.
Every tile a cherished thought,
In the mosaic, love is caught.

Time is gentle, yet it flies,
In every glance and soft goodbyes.
Moments cherished, small and grand,
Each one placed by careful hand.

Through every twist and woven path,
We create a harmony that lasts.
In the chaos, we find our plot,
An artful frame for what we've sought.

Every smile, a piece of light,
Shines amidst our shared delight.
Together crafting joy and pain,
In this mosaic, we remain.

The Canvas of Connection

Brushstrokes bold on blank expanse,
Our hearts paint with every chance.
Hues of laughter, shades of sighs,
United truths that never lie.

Each moment splashed in colors bright,
A canvas holding day and night.
In strokes of hope, in lines of grace,
Connections bloom in time and space.

From muted tones to vibrant gleam,
A masterpiece born from a dream.
Together we blend, merge, and sway,
Creating worlds in our own way.

The brush in hand, we dare to claim,
Every passion, every name.
On this canvas, love paints free,
A portrait of you and me.

In every layer, depth we find,
Stories woven, intertwined.
This canvas speaks, our truth laid bare,
In every stroke, we deeply care.

Beneath the Surface of Us

Ripples echo, hidden deep,
Awakening feelings we keep.
The surface glimmers, a gentle guise,
Beneath it swells a world of sighs.

What lies beneath, a treasure trove,
Secrets whispered, hearts in grove.
With every tide, the truth draws near,
In the depths, we have no fear.

Hands entwined, we dive below,
Discovering currents, ebb and flow.
In silent spaces, love can breathe,
Water's embrace, our souls wreathe.

The depths are rich, with dreams adorned,
In darkened waters, we're reborn.
Together navigating what we find,
In every splash, our hearts aligned.

Beyond the surface, we explore,
Each layer peeled, revealing more.
In the depths of us, we trust,
Bound forever, rise we must.

Pockets of Joy

In the quiet of dawn, we find,
Little treasures intertwined.
A smile, a laugh, a fleeting glance,
Moments held in a joyful dance.

Sunshine whispers through the trees,
Carrying laughter on the breeze.
Soft echoes of a child at play,
Painting colors on a gray day.

In every hug, a spark ignites,
Binding us in pure delights.
We gather moments, small and bright,
Creating warmth in darkest night.

Chocolate kisses and lemonade,
Silly games in the afternoon shade.
These pockets of joy, a sweet embrace,
Forever cherished, time can't erase.

So let's collect them, you and I,
Moments that teach our spirits to fly.
With each heartbeat, together we grow,
In these pockets of joy, love will flow.

The Tides of Togetherness

Like waves that crash upon the shore,
Together, we share so much more.
With hands held tight, we'll brave the storm,
In the tides of life, we'll keep warm.

Each ebb and flow, a rhythm divine,
In our hearts, a bright, steady line.
Through trials faced and challenges met,
Our bond remains, with no regret.

The moon's soft glow guides our way,
In unison, we sway and play.
From sunrise's blush to twilight's call,
Together, we rise, together, we fall.

When shadows loom and fears arise,
We'll stand as one, with steady ties.
For love is the compass of the sea,
In the tides of togetherness, we'll always be.

So let the waves dance wild and free,
With open hearts, we'll find the key.
For in this ocean, vast and wide,
We'll navigate it all side by side.

A Compass for Two

When paths diverge and choices loom,
With you, my heart finds its room.
Together, we'll chart unknown seas,
Guided by love's gentle breeze.

A compass spins in trust's embrace,
In your eyes, I find my place.
With every step, we weave our tale,
With laughter bright and dreams that sail.

Through forests deep, and mountains high,
We walk, with stars as our guide.
In the map of life, we'll make our way,
With hands connected, come what may.

The horizon stretches, vast and grand,
But together, we boldly stand.
With love as our beacon, shining true,
A compass forever, just for two.

Let's explore the world, hand in hand,
In leaps of faith, together we'll land.
With every heartbeat, every sigh,
This compass leads us, you and I.

Reveries of Nostalgia

In quiet moments, memories stir,
Whispers of laughter, heartbeats purr.
Old photographs, pages of time,
In the garden of dreams, we still climb.

Each echo speaks of days gone by,
Beneath the vast and open sky.
Sweet fragrances of faded bloom,
In reveries, we find our room.

Childhood games and summer's glow,
Time slips gently, like melting snow.
With every sigh, an old song plays,
In the tapestry of yesterday's rays.

Those lingering glances, the warmth we felt,
In the heart's chamber, emotions melt.
So let's cherish what once was true,
In the reveries of nostalgia, me and you.

As twilight wraps the day in gold,
Our stories, sweet and softly told.
In the fabric of time, we'll forever weave,
These precious moments, we won't leave.

Resilience in Shared Struggles

In shadows deep, we find our way,
Together strong, we face the fray.
With open hearts, we lift the veil,
In shared struggles, we shall prevail.

Each tear a river, each laugh a light,
We walk as one, our spirits bright.
Through storms and trials, we hold tight,
With courage, we shall win this fight.

In unity, we rise anew,
Hand in hand, we'll see it through.
Resilience blooms where hope is fed,
In every word that's left unsaid.

From ashes stirred, we build a bridge,
Together stepping, hearts won't frigid.
With every setback, we'll ignite,
Our spirits soar to greater heights.

A tapestry of dreams we weave,
In love and strength, we truly believe.
With every heartbeat, every sigh,
Together, we will touch the sky.

The Garden We Cultivate

In gentle hands, we plant the seeds,
Nurturing dreams, fulfilling needs.
With every drop of sun and rain,
We cultivate joy, ease the pain.

Petals unfurl with colors bright,
In this garden, pure delight.
Together we tend, our roots entwined,
Each blossom a story, love defined.

We prune away the fears that grow,
With every friend, we learn and know.
In shadows cast, we find our grace,
In every challenge, we embrace.

The fragrance lingers in the air,
Each moment cherished, moments rare.
From tiny sprouts to trees so grand,
In our garden, life's carefully planned.

A harvest shared, our bounties bright,
With laughter echoing through the night.
In unity, we flourish bold,
In this garden, love unfolds.

Stars Aligned in Unity

Beneath the sky, where stars convene,
In cosmic dance, a sight serene.
United spirits weave their fate,
In harmony, we illuminate.

Each twinkle tells a tale of old,
Of dreams and hopes, of hearts consoled.
Together crossing paths so bright,
In the vastness, we share our light.

With every wish upon a star,
We reach for peace, we travel far.
In unity, our dreams take flight,
Bound by the threads of pure delight.

The night sky shimmers with our song,
In each connection, we belong.
With whispered prayers and laughter shared,
In this vast cosmos, we are prepared.

Stars aligned, we walk this road,
Together carrying love's great load.
In every heartbeat, every sigh,
We find our place beneath the sky.

The Sewing Circle of Affection

In a circle warm, we gather round,
With threads of love, our hearts are bound.
Each stitch a memory, soft and true,
In shared moments, our spirits grew.

With laughter woven, tears displayed,
In needle and thread, our fears betray.
We patch the seams of troubled minds,
With every stitch, affection finds.

A fabric rich with colors bright,
In every piece, a story's light.
Together forming quilts of grace,
A tapestry of each embrace.

As seasons change and time goes by,
In our circle, love won't die.
Each knot a promise, every seam,
In this circle, we weave our dream.

Hand in hand, we share our plight,
With gentle care, we hold each night.
In every stitch, our love we share,
The sewing circle, rich and rare.

Milton Keynes UK
Ingram Content Group UK Ltd.
UKHW022003131124
451149UK00013B/994

9 789916 867532